Turtles

A Compare and Contrast Book

by Cher Vataloro

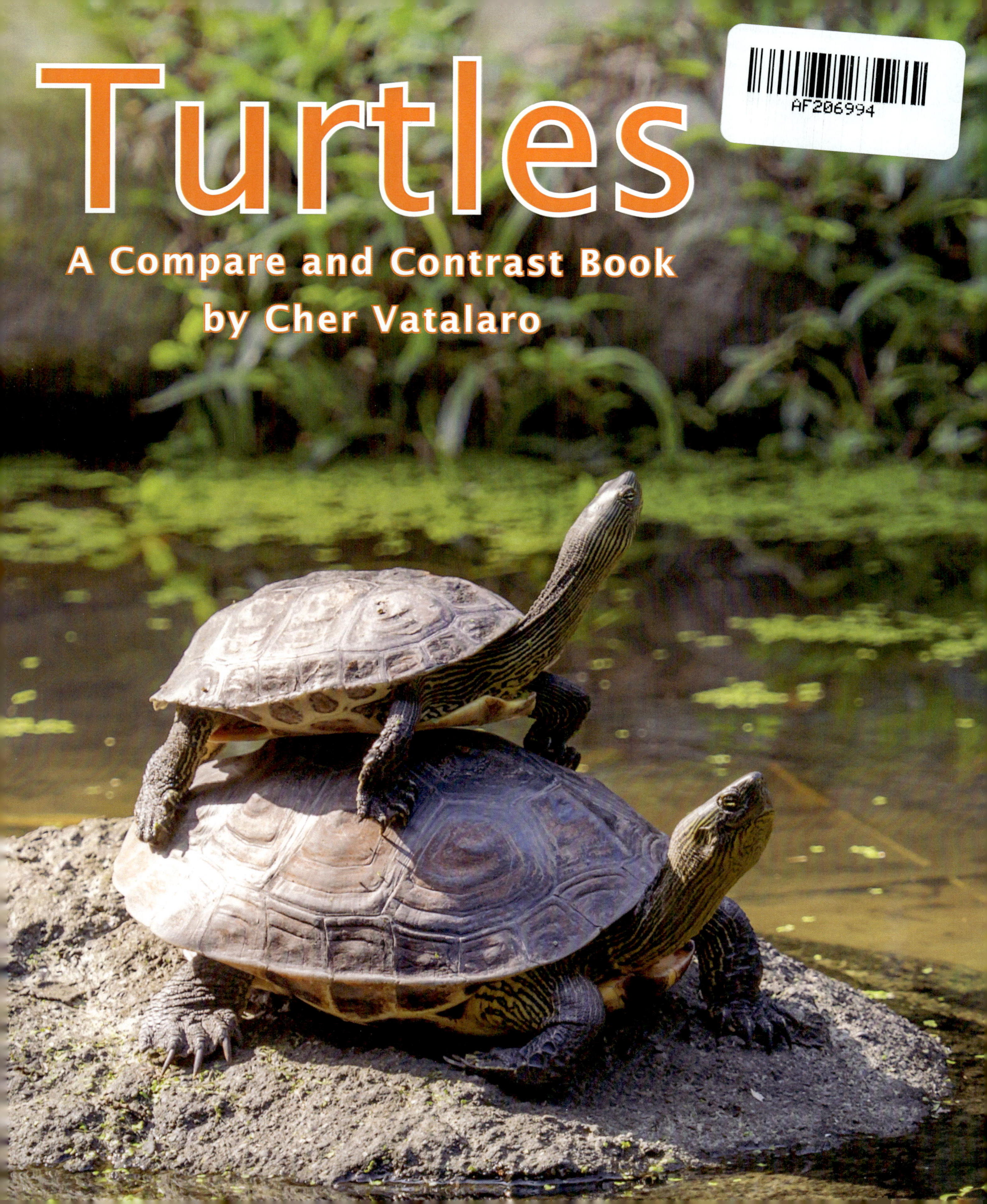

loggerhead sea turtle

"Turtle" is the term typically used for all turtles and tortoises.

Turtles are reptiles. There are over 300 different species of turtles that live all over the world except for Antarctica. They live in all kinds of habitats from the salty oceans to dry deserts.

Diamondback terrapin

Mojave desert tortoise

Galapagos tortoise

The defining feature of a turtle is its hard shell. The top of the shell is called the carapace and the bottom is called the plastron.

red-eared slider

plastron of red-footed tortoise

plastron of painted turtle

The shell is part of its skeleton and is made from bone. Turtles cannot leave their shell. They are attached to it by their spine. As the animals grow, so do their shells, just like our bones grow as we grow.

The bone is covered with scutes that are made from keratin, just like our hair and fingernails.

scutes: African spurred tortoise

scutes: red-footed tortoise

They do not have teeth
but use strong beaks
to eat their food.

African spurred tortoise

Hawksbill sea turtle

Aldabra tortoise

Galapagos tortoise

Seychelles tortoise

Hermann tortoise

Tortoises are herbivores, meaning they only eat plants.

True turtles are omnivores. They eat both plants and meat.

eastern box turtle

Hawskbill sea turtle

All turtles breathe oxygen from the air.

Even if swimming in a pond, river, lake, or ocean, they still need to come to the surface of the water to breathe air.

loggerhead sea turtle

Chinese pond turtle

All turtles are cold-blooded. You can often spot turtles like these painted turtles or the Aldabra giant tortoise basking in the sun to warm up.

Sea turtles migrate to warmer waters when the ocean waters start to cool down for winter.

Some turtles can pull their heads completely or mostly into their shells for protection from predators.

box turtle

desert tortoise

snapping turtle

Sea turtles, like this loggerhead, cannot pull their heads into their shells at all.

Like most reptiles, turtles lay eggs. Turtles that spend all or most of their time in the water must crawl onto land to lay eggs.

Depending on the type of turtle, the female may lay eggs in burrows, deep in sand, dirt, or even in leaves.

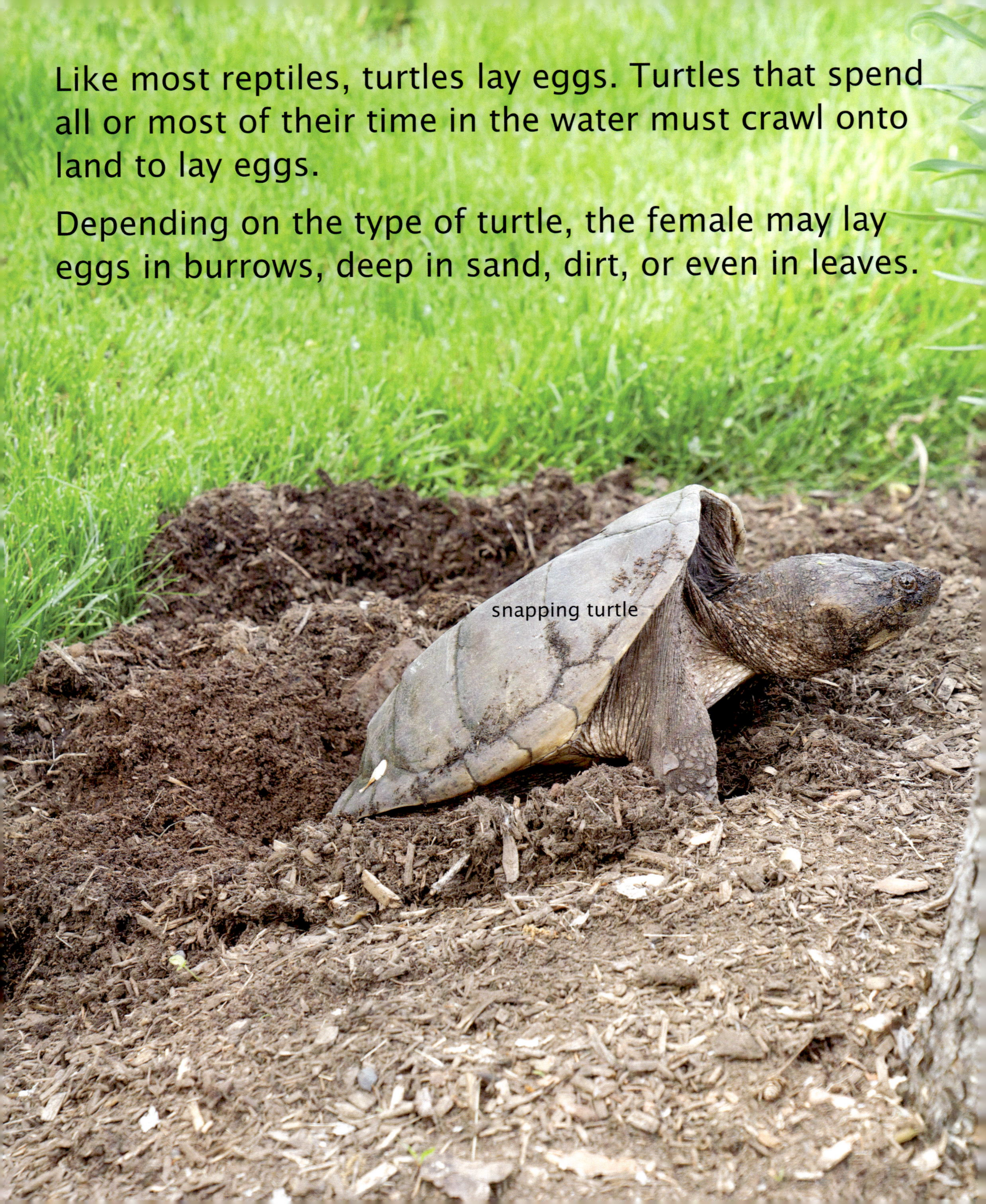

loggerhead sea turtle

tortoise

red-eared slider

Tortoises only live on land. They have rounded, dome-like shells.

Seychelles tortoise

leopard tortoise

gopher tortoise

True turtles are adapted for life in the water. They have flat, thin, streamlined shells to help them swim. Their shells are also lighter than tortoise shells.

painted turtle

red-eared slider

Of course, there are exceptions to most rules. Box turtles have domed shells and pancake tortoises, have flat shells!

Tortoises have columnar hind limbs and feet—like elephant legs and feet. They have claws on their front feet to help them dig burrows.

True turtles have flipper-like limbs and webbed feet to help them move through water. Most turtles that go back and forth between water and land have claws on their feet to help them move on land.

Sea turtles only have flippers.

Turtles come in all different shapes and sizes and live in many different habitats from deserts to the ocean.

green sea turtle

wood turtle

South American snapping turtle

terrapins

Galapagos tortoise

For Creative Minds

Turtle Feet and Legs: What Can You Tell?

What can you tell by a turtle's feet and legs?

1a

1b

1c

Answers: 1a: webs with claws tells us that the turtle lives in both water and on land, 1b: columnar legs (like an elephant's) with claws for digging tells us the turtle (tortoise) lives only on land, 1c: legs that are flippers for swimming tells us it's a sea turtle.

Match the Turtle to its Habitat

1

2

3

4

A

B

C

D

Answers: 1-C: ocean, 2-D: desert, 3-A: pond, 4-B: woods near water

Turtle True or False?

Can you tell which statements are true and which are false? Answers are below.

1	Sea turtles lay their eggs in the ocean.
2	Turtles, tortoises, and terrapins are all considered turtles. They are reptiles.
3	Most, but not all, turtles live in water and on land.
4	Turtles have very sharp teeth.
5	Turtles live in all kinds of habitats all over the world except for Antarctica.
6	Turtles crawl out of their shells and get new ones as they grow.
7	Turtle scutes and human fingernails are both made of keratin.
8	Turtles only eat plants (herbivore).
9	Turtles are cold-blooded.
10	Tortoises only live on land.

Answers: 1: False-all turtles lay eggs on land. 2: True. 3: True. 4: False-turtles have beaks and no teeth. 5: True. 6: False: turtle shells are part of their skeleton. 7: True. 8: False-some turtles eat plants and others eat meat or both plants and meat. 9: True. 10: True

Turtle Body Parts

Identify the turtle body parts using the vocabulary list. Answers are below.

beak	the hard, curved part of an animal's mouth
carapace (care-a-pace)	the top of a turtle's shell
claws	the sharp, curved end of toes
nostrils	the openings into a nose
plastron (pla-stron)	the bottom part of a turtle's shell
scutes (skoots)	the large bony plates on a turtle's carapace

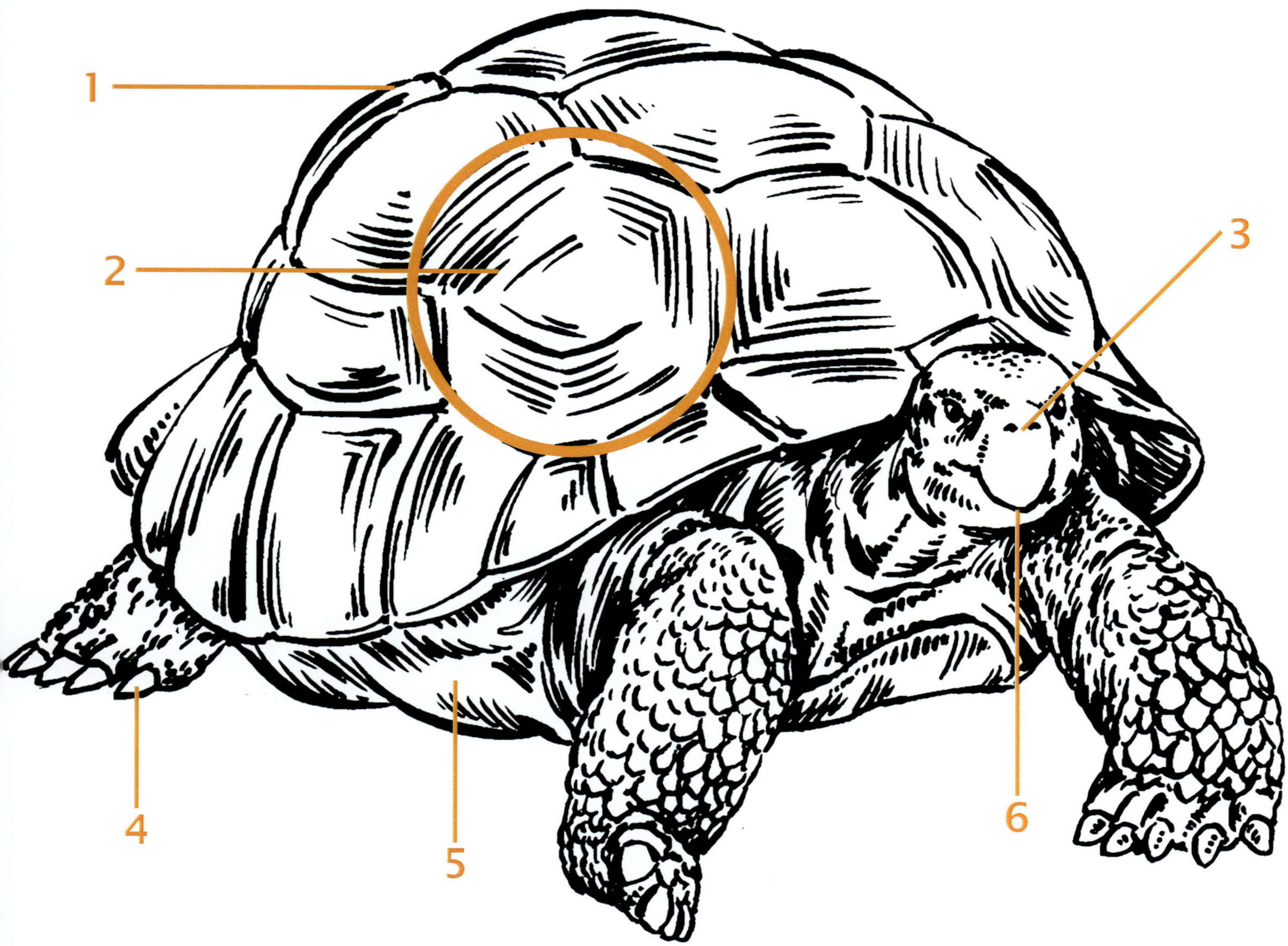

Answers: 1: carapace, 2: scutes, 3: nostrils, 4: claws, 5: plastron, 6: beak

Thanks to Kristi Dodds, Learning Coordinator at the Woodland Park Zoo for verifying the information in this book.

All photographs are licensed through Adobe Stock Photos or Shutterstock.

Library of Congress Cataloging-in-Publication Data

Names: Vatalaro, Cher, 1988- author.
Title: Turtles : a compare and contrast book / by Cher Vatalaro.
Description: Mt. Pleasant, SC : Arbordale Publishing, LLC, [2023] | Includes bibliographical references.
Identifiers: LCCN 2022036982 (print) | LCCN 2022036983 (ebook) | ISBN 9781643519951 (paperback) | ISBN 9781638170143 (interactive dual-language, read along) | ISBN 9781638170525 (epub) | ISBN 9781638170334 (adobe pdf)
Subjects: LCSH: Turtles--Juvenile literature.
Classification: LCC QL666.C5 V38 2023 (print) | LCC QL666.C5 (ebook) | DDC 597.92--dc23/eng/20220804
LC record available at https://lccn.loc.gov/2022036982
LC ebook record available at https://lccn.loc.gov/2022036983

Translated into Spanish: ***Tortugas: Un libro de comparaciones y contrastes***
Spanish paperback ISBN: 9781638172949
Spanish ePub ISBN: 9781638173069
Spanish PDF ebook ISBN: 9781638173021
Dual-language read-along available online at www.fathomreads.com

English Lexile® Level: 590L

Bibliography:

"African Pancake Tortoise." Smithsonian's National Zoo, 3 July 2019, nationalzoo.si.edu/animals/african-pancake-tortoise.

"Dermochelys Coriacea (Leatherback Sea Turtle)." Animal Diversity Web, 2019, animaldiversity.org/accounts/Dermochelys_coriacea/.

"Galápagos Tortoise | San Diego Zoo Animals & Plants." Sandiegozoo.org, 2015, animals.sandiegozoo.org/animals/galapagos-tortoise.

Hamny, The. "Types of Turtles (14 Families, and 351 Species)." The Hamny, 8 Jan. 2022, thehamny.com/types-of-turtles/.

Niedzielski, Steven. "Terrapene Carolina (Florida Box Turtle)." Animal Diversity Web, animaldiversity.org/accounts/Terrapene_carolina/.

"What's the Difference between a Turtle and a Tortoise?" Encyclopedia Britannica, www.britannica.com/story/whats-the-difference-between-a-turtle-and-a-tortoise.

"What's the Difference between Turtles and Tortoises?" Nashvillezoo.org, 2017, www.nashvillezoo.org/our-blog/posts/turtles-vs-tortoises.

Printed in the US
This product conforms to CPSIA 2008

Arbordale Publishing
Mt. Pleasant, SC 29464
www.ArbordalePublishing.com